Spirit of Fire

Spirit of Fire

CAROLYN ASKAR

A Nadder Book
ELEMENT BOOKS LTD

© Carolyn Askar 1983
First published in Great Britain 1983 by
Element Books Ltd
The Old Brewery, Tisbury, Salisbury
Wiltshire

Printed in Great Britain by
Biddles Limited, Guildford
Cover illustration by Alison Chapman
Text and Cover design by Humphrey Stone

ISBN 0 906 540 43 7

Contents

Spirit of Fire	3
The Lighthouse	9
Picture Her	11
A Life	13
At the Root of the Breath	14
Haiku I	15
Patterns and Cycles	16
Loose Buckles	18
Buckling up	19
Haiku II	20
Haiku III	21
My Faith	22
Synthesis	23
The Letter I	24
Cultivation	27
Clouds	28
Haiku IV	29
Crystal Clear	31
The Other Self	32
Through the Child's Eyes	34
Haiku V	35
Song of the Gnostic	36
The Building	38

The Spaces in Between	39
Haiku VI	40
Elemental	41
Decline	42
World Image	43
When we are Gone	44
Material	46
Human Mayflies	47
The Touch	49
The Mountain in Perspective	50

Illustrations by

HULY ASKAR

ALISON CHAPMAN

PATRICK QUINLAN

MEHRAN SABETYAN

STEPHEN SILVER

Acknowledgements

I should like to thank the dear friends who have kindly allowed me to reproduce their paintings and drawings in this book. Their illustrations appear on the following pages: Huly Askar, 1, 12, 33, 37; Alison Chapman, 5, 10 and verse, 20, 21; Patrick Quinlan, 8, 17, 25, 30; Mehran Sabetyan, 45; Stephen Silver, 26, 48.

Thanks are also due to Expansion Publications, for allowing me to retain Copyright on the title poem, which appeared in the April issue of their magazine.

This book is dedicated to:
HULY
MAEDÉE, ABBAS AND STEPHEN
GRETA AND RAJAN
THE AMRITA TRUST

Introduction

Man, in his ageless quest for understanding, has produced so many ideas and theories, so many philosophies and doctrines to explain his joys and distract from his suffering. It is rare, however, to come across an idea which is not an idea, a doctrine of no doctrine, a philosophy which is just a way of being.

In Spirit of Fire, Carolyn Askar shows us some of the ways she sees and tastes the experience of life. The book is not about a point of view; rather it is a synthesis of her inner vision, beyond the personal, which expresses a simple and unshakeable truth, a reverence for life.

STEPHEN SILVER M.RAD.A.

Spirit of Fire

In a circle of wax
the candles stood round,
awaiting the match
that couldn't be found.
Each separate colour
awaited that sound –
the all-powerful scratch of the match.

    Rainbows of colour
    dividing the swarms
    of pure wax candles
    with too many thorns,
    varying fragrances
    odd shapes and sizes,
    pure wax candles
    in many disguises
    stand in a circle,
    a circle of wax,
    awaiting the click
    and the scratch of the match.

As the match was struck
they began to melt,
and no-one can say
what pain was felt.
The flame was revealed
as the colours were peeled –
and every last flame was yellow.

      Rainbows of colour
      dividing the swarms
      of candles and people
      with too many thorns,
      varying fragrances
      odd shapes and sizes,
      candles and people
      in human disguises
      stand in a circle,
      a circle of wax.
      As the yellow flames burn,
      the wax fills the cracks.

The wicks burned bright
and softened the night;
and hearts burned bright,
warmed by the light;
then slowly it dawned,
as hearts grew mellow,
that every last flame was yellow.

    Rainbows of colour
    dividing the swarms
    of candles and people
    with too many thorns;
    varying fragrances
    odd shapes and sizes,
    pure human souls
    in many disguises
    stand in a circle
    a circle of fire,
    and human hearts burn
    with the spirit of fire.

Then candles were kindled
all over the earth,
lighting our world
to its future re-birth,
with yellow flames glowing
in the hearts of men, knowing
the kindling spirit of peace.

    All the candles were nothing,
    nothing but tallow,
    but the spirits soared
    in flames of yellow,
    and the universe swelled
    and grew bright with light,
    as peace and love
    abolished the night.
    See through the rainbows,
    rise with the fire,
    for the universe glows
    with the spirit of fire.

The Lighthouse

The world
gathered up her skirts,
and with a mighty intake of breath,
rolled
in a towering wave
towards the shores of eternity.

Before
the oily skin could split,
splashing forth its contents in a foam of chaos,
the Master
appeared, standing on the crest
of a higher invisible wave of luminescence.

The gross tide
checked, standing poised to burst,
as the winds streamed forth from the barrier of light.
Thus locked
they remained, till the gradual dawning
of recognition.

The wave then
ebbed, with a self-conscious jostle
and splash, back to a choppy ocean.

The Master
shook his head
and smiled at his clumsy children.

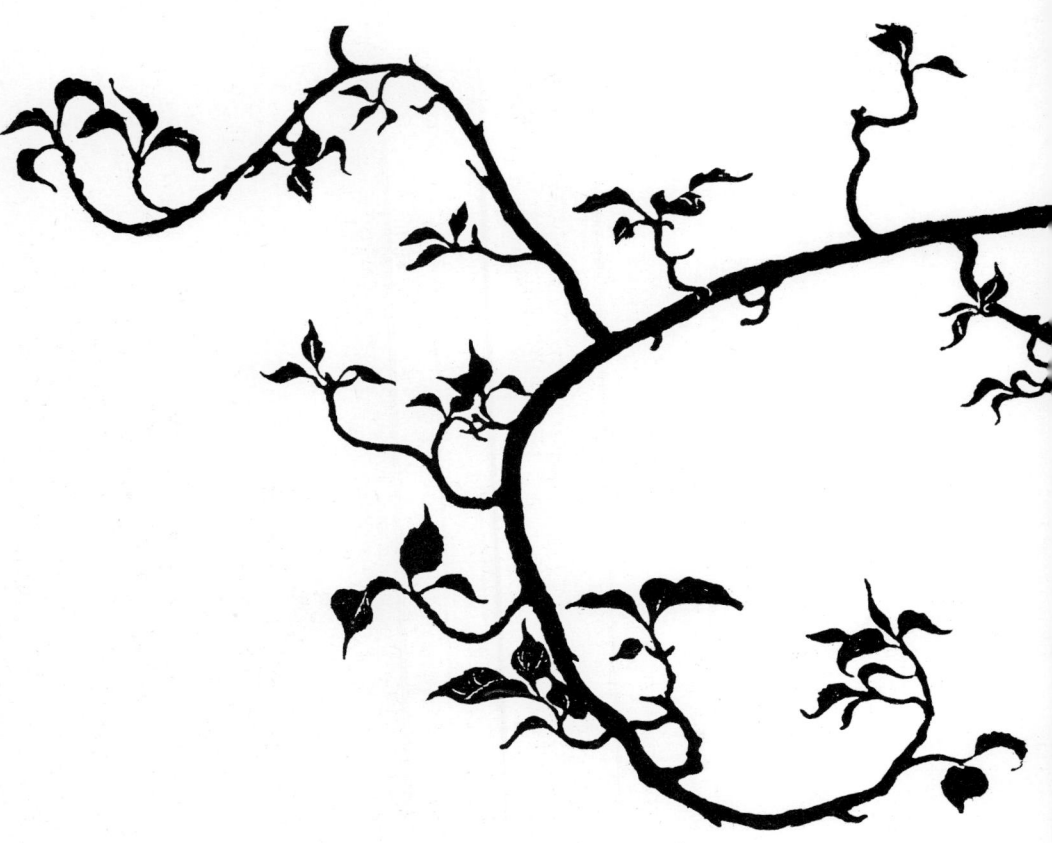

Motionless evening branches:
                      Dancing.
Rhythm forms the rose.
All God His joyous creation:
                      Dancing;
Passing the golden thread from hand to hand.

                      A. C.

Picture Her

Her windswept hair
mingles with the branches.
From her loamy feet
the grasses grow.
Her hands wipe clean
your windows and caress
tight buds to open.
Her heart beats to your echo.
She is life and so are you.

Her mind drives clouds
and challenges the wind.
Your hearth's sun-warmed
by her smile. Her eyes
look down from velvet dark.
Her muscle powers
your womb to bear its fruit.
She sheds her "s", and still
♦he is life and ♦he is you.

A Life

In the beginning
was a life.
The body grew
straight and tall,
and the mind
was a bud,
that waited
for the spring.
The winds blew
to the corners of the mind,
and with the sun,
unfoldment began.

The flower opened
to reveal a stamen
leading to deep
recesses and the root.
As the sunlight
filtered to the core,
a shudder of being
passed through the plant.

Time passed.
The sun grew hot;
the petals stretched wide,
centre thrusting towards the light –
till the flower dried
to delicate transparency,
leaving the bulb
to fuse with its source,
– and await the next bloom.

At the Root of the Breath

At the root of the breath
is a sigh,
the soft blown sigh
of humanity.
Exhaled on her breath
are her woes,
her unending air
of melancholy.
The breath is almost
expired,
the Piscean gamut
out-run.
Prepare to refill
the lungs,
for Aquarian air
is strong.

Haiku I

Friendship is listening
to familiar echoes from
those who understand.

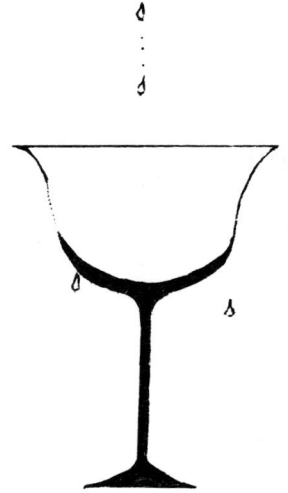

A chalice is for
filling to the brim with love
till all thirst is quenched.

Patterns and Cycles

Groups of people assembled
striving hard to be friends,
ignoring old scars
from previous wars,
they tried to make amends;
but memories flashed by
giving the lie
and they let slip words to offend.

Heads of state assembled
to talk of the horrors of war,
till every last nation
pledged co-operation, –
non-violence for evermore;
but the missiles rolled by
giving the lie
and they slipped back behind closed doors.

Then the armies assembled,
(each believing the other was wrong)
prayed for power to their will
and a licence to kill,
God cried when he heard their song;
for the widows filed by,
wiping their eye,
and their suffering vigil grew long.

Loose Buckles

1, 2,
weapons new
3, 4,
let's make more
5, 6,
something ticks
7, 8,
not too late
9, 10,
a quarrel, and then
11, 12,
caution shelve
13, 14,
danger courting
15, 16,
sanity drifting
17, 18,
patience abating
19, 20,
planet's empty

Buckling up

1, 2,
friendships new
3, 4,
let's make more
5, 6,
détente clicks
7, 8,
co-operate
9, 10,
breathe again
11, 12,
dig and delve
13, 14,
new ways sorting
15, 16,
obstacles shifting
17, 18,
better times waiting
19, 20,
no plates empty

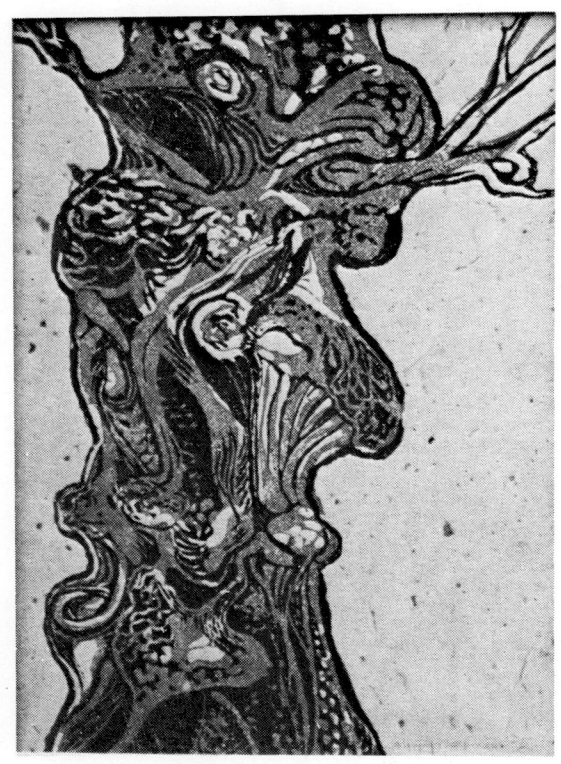

Haiku II

Internal decor
heavy pot full of dull earth
sprouting greenery.

        Slowly slithering
        green and earthbound emotion
        serpent of envy.

Haiku III

Dark glowing embers
blown to a fiery furnace
revisited love.

        The first of many
        unknown facets of the mind
        sixth sense acknowledged.

My Faith

My faith
lies in the cracks
between religions.

The prism of truth
refracts light
in many colours
of equal validity
and brightness.

To be
free to wander
through the rays
and discover
again and again
the same
white brilliance,
is to rejoice
in the wonders,
the enigmas,
and faithful reflections
of love.

Synthesis

See the blue smoke curl
rising, filmy-veiled,
expanding its fragrance
to dispersal in space.

See the ray of light,
shafting from the sky,
grounding its current
of energy in the earth.

See the truth emerge,
shining through the heart,
reflecting love's ray
to fill the world with peace.

The Letter 'I'

Imagination
>uses thoughts
>as stepping stones
>to leap one stage beyond.

Inspiration
>is the touch
>of a greater mind breathed in.

Intuition
>is the message
>absorbed through the heart.

Instinct
>is the movement
>of information in the gut.

Ideas
>are the sparks
>that can be welded into light.

Incarnation
>is the vehicle
>and the shackle of the soul.

I
>is the initial
>letter of the word of man.

I
>the Identity.

>When *I* expands
>the soul is free
>to join the pool of love.

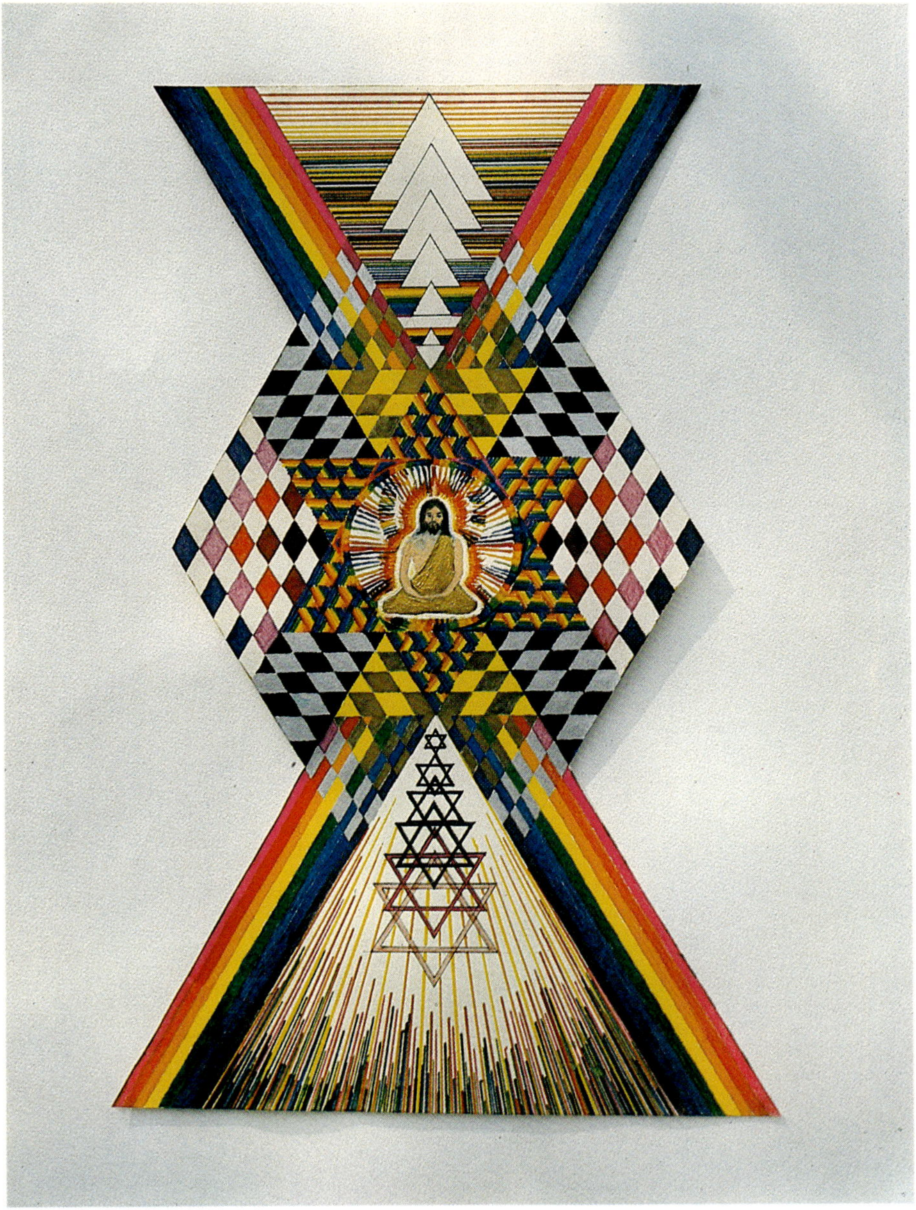

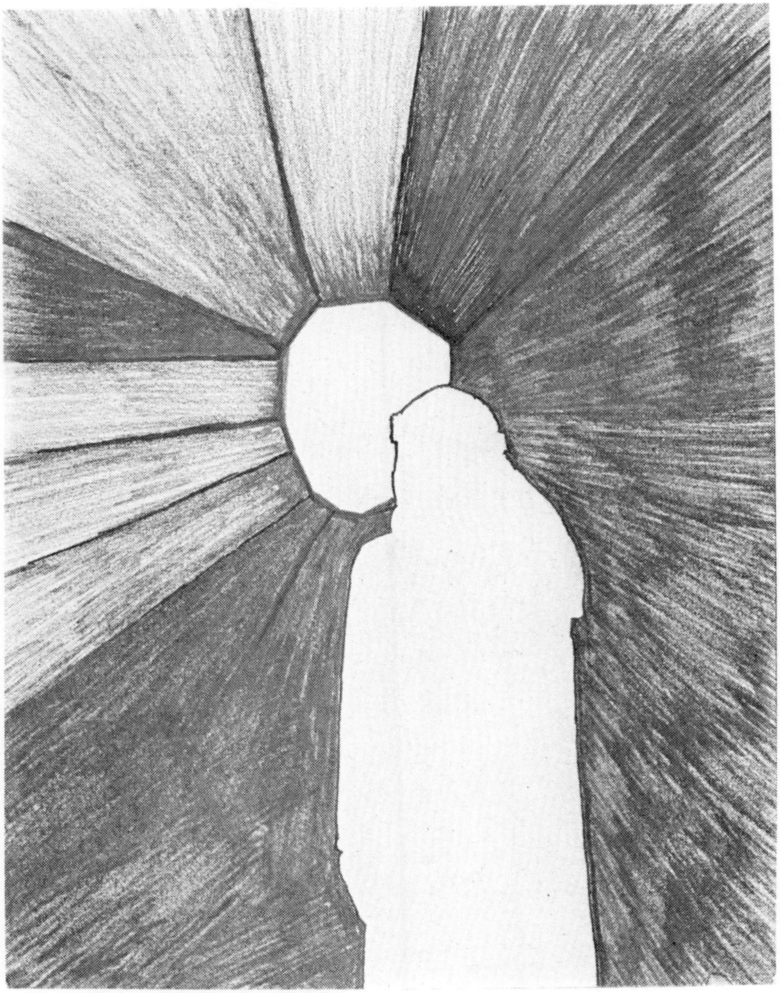

Cultivation

You refresh us.
We drink at Your pool.
With secret balm
You soothe and cool
the fevered mind.

Cradled in Your arms
we watch the earth
moving through time
tracing the path
of Your design.

Cast seeds germinate
in fertile plains
of consciousness
where Your love rains
from clouds divine.

Clouds

Ominous columns
rise over
the horizon;
then fan out
in batallions,
sped by the wind.

They challenge the sun.

Our life-source smiles
sublimely,
acquiesces,
and is blacked out
by dense nimbus
raining despair.

The bright green valley
turns sombre
and darkens,
despite the knowledge
of the sun,
hidden from view.

Storms of dark thoughts
and shadows
will blow over.
Meanwhile we grow,
through rainfall,
nearer the sun.

Haiku IV

Dark clouds that move like
a quilt over paradise
rain into the mind.

Dry thoughts warmed by love
create the sparks of spirit
that chase clouds away.

Shaking off moisture
and lifting heart towards heat
allows thoughts to dry.

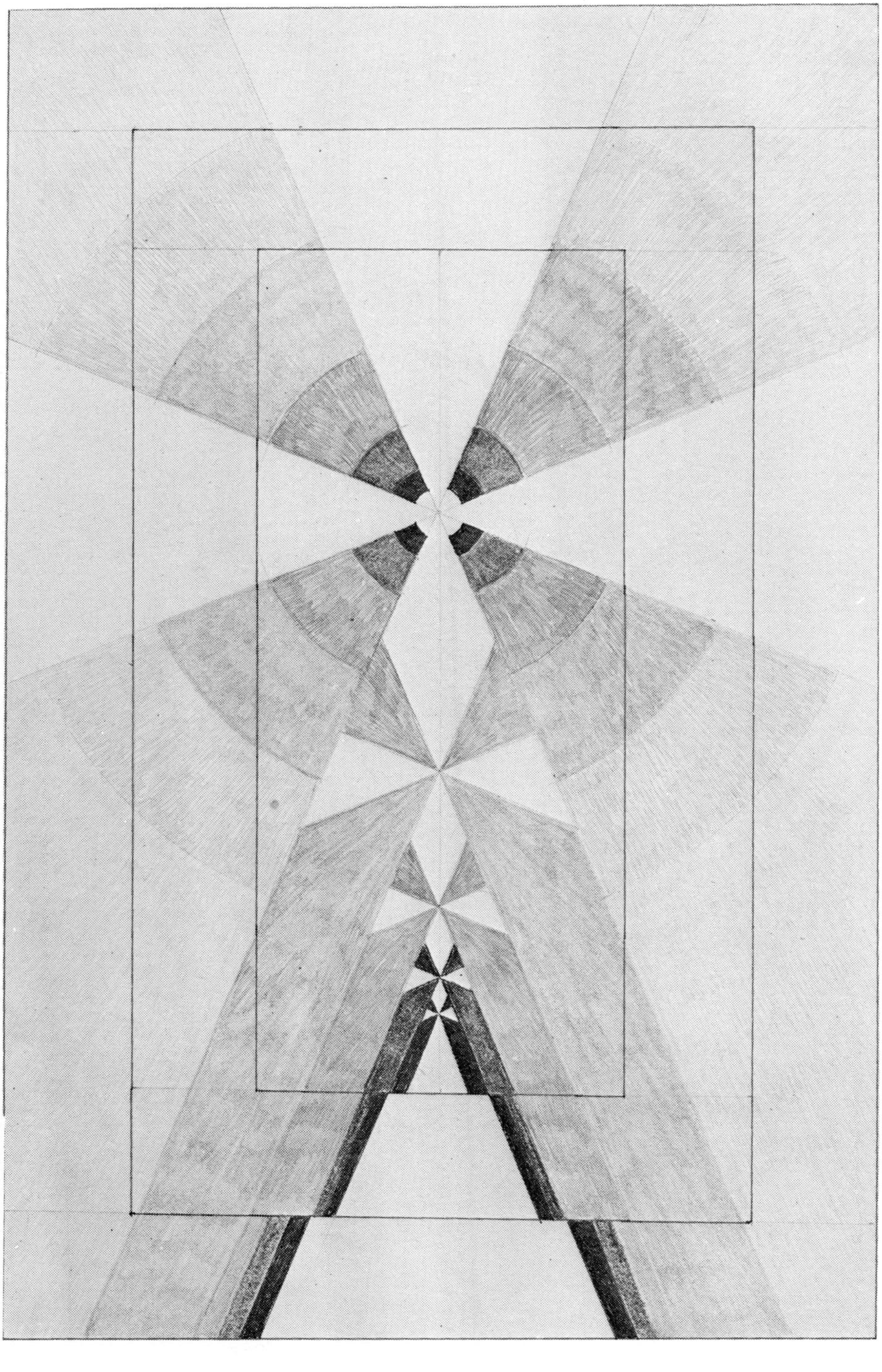

Crystal Clear

Clear as crystal
bright as the sun,
the prism of simple
truth was begun.

Coloured refraction
of the white lance
distorted the image
in dizzy dance.

The mirror of maya
reflected illusion,
compounding angles
and causing confusion.

The Other Self

The eyes shut,
and through the window
of the head
appears
an incomplete
painting-by-numbers.
A 'Dali' woman.

The patches of colour
fill, slowly,
floating nearer
on a backcloth of light,
commanding attention.

The face,
unprompted,
smiles response
to the benign impulse.

Something flows between them.

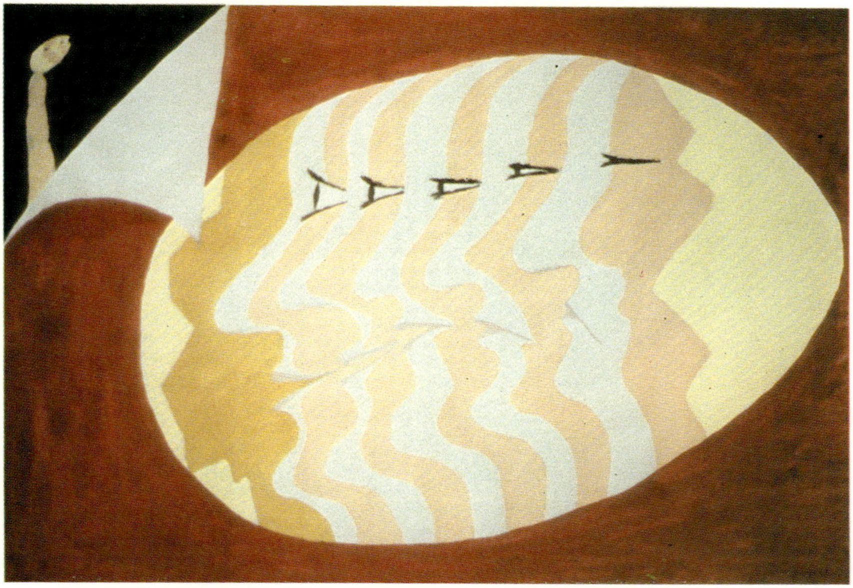

Through the Child's Eyes

"What do you think God is?"
we asked the boy of seven.

Retreating behind his puckered brow
and diving inside his green-grey eyes,
he fished deep for his answer.

We held our breath.

Surfacing, he exhaled
in a clear stream:

"God is a spirit
that wanted to make
something really fabulous.
And He did it.
And He has promised
to look after it forever."

Haiku V

Children's questions are
for stimulating adults
to seek true answers.

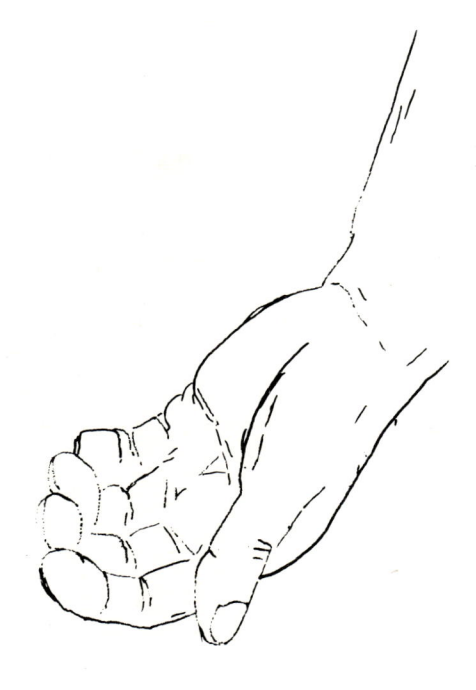

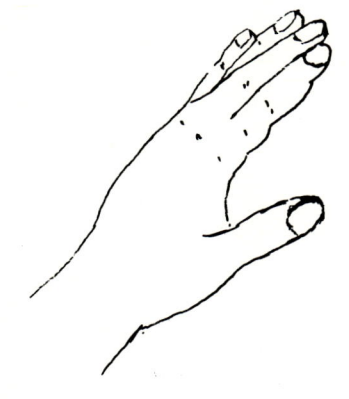

Parental duty
is knowing when to let go
and how to support.

Song of the Gnostic

Tap tap:
The daily woodpeckers
chip away
at the bark of his calm.

Knock knock:
The man who can't find
the friend within himself
raps at his stillness
for understanding.

Bang bang:
The prisoner of his own illusions
seeks to break free
via the gnostic's walls.

Scratch scratch:
The soul who has peeped
through the window
begs admittance.

But
the reverberating boom
that resounds within,
before the door is struck,
is the one
he leaps to answer.

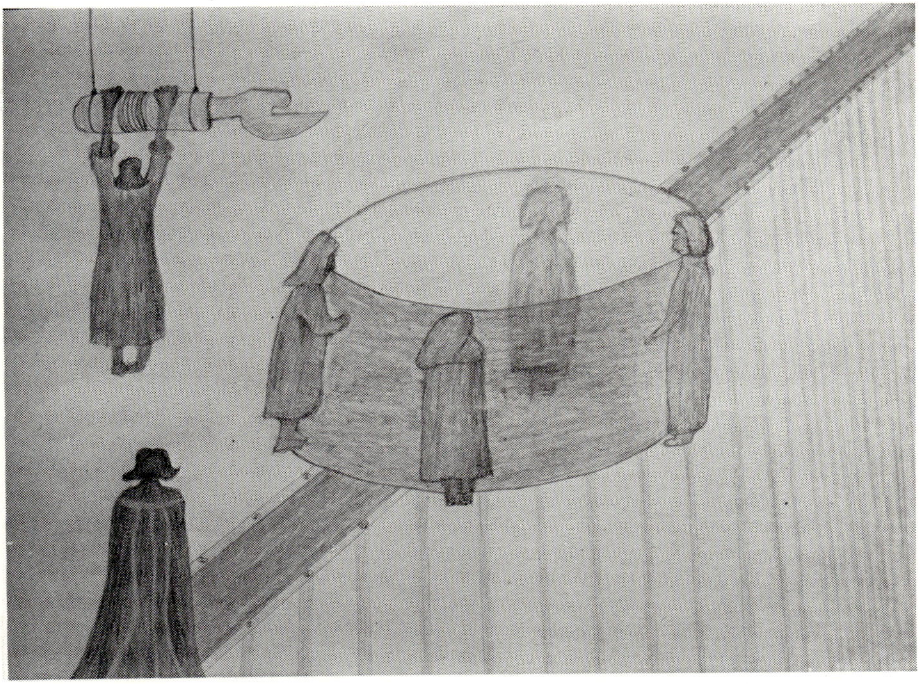

The Building
(for the performer)

On the springboard
poised for action
ponder options
of direction.

Choose a purpose
and a function,
find a channel
for expression.

Working through
communication,
build a platform
for the action.

The Spaces in Between

(for the performer)

Actions and sounds
pause in silence
for listening.

Thoughts extend
leaving spaces
for feeling.

Clouds drift apart
and between, light
is streaming.

Senses expand
into stillness
for receiving.

Inside the calm
intuition
is flowing.

Inside the heart
understanding
is growing.

Haiku VI

(for the performer)

Refracting white light
into rainbow expression
the artist's prism.

Fiery flames fuelled by
power of concentration
the artist's furnace.

Through polished windows
shining with life's reflection
the artist's lantern.

Focusing the beam
to transmit inspiration
the artist's spotlight.

Elemental

'Water' poets,
sometimes airy, rising,
trail emotion
to drip and splash
with wet garments
impeding the spirit.
In 'natural' descriptions,
dried out by sunlight
and clear breezes,
that bleach images
and lift to wholesome heat.
They are often, however,
sucked back to moisture
by something unresolved,
that flounders in mud
– far from Plath's fire.
She, consumed by dryness,
fanning her passions
(with love-pores blocked,)
filled her verse
with a fiery-spirit,
– whose intensity exploded.

Water flows freely.
Fire's elusive.
Will air suffice?
Or alchemy?

Decline

Passing shadows
etching wrinkles
summer's end
growing cold.
Passing into
autumn shadow
vibrance spent
growing old.

Is there time
to leap on wagon
filled with those
in twilight flood?

Feel the chillness
of the stillness
slowing down
congealing blood.
Pink to greyness
left behind
immobile thoughts
fill the mind.
Song of sadness
giving up
summer madness
drain the cup.
Thirst is quenched
day is done
fade to darkness
winter's come.

World Image

The colours pulse
with solid brilliance,
charged with energy
in our vision;
a mirrored glimpse
of our potential.

Smudging outlines
blurr the image
and the spectrum dims
as power runs out.
The brightness fades
with our ebb.

When we are Gone

When we are gone, please speak of us;
Do not fear.
The words which we have spoken
Will remain.
We will be here.
Don't bury us
Or burn us with our bones;
Keep us alive
Forever in your consciousness
We will survive.

Our love is all.
We are the things we do,
The words we speak,
The touch we.warm,
The love we give and take.
The contact,
Good or bad,
With fellow man,
Is our own scent
rubbed off along life's path.

Accept our mortal bones
Back in the earth;
But keep our universal
Spirit glowing,
In colours that are ours,
Yet shared by all –
In tones so multi-varied
That we think,
Mistakenly, that we are separate.

We are the individual shades and hues
Of one continuous woven strand of life.

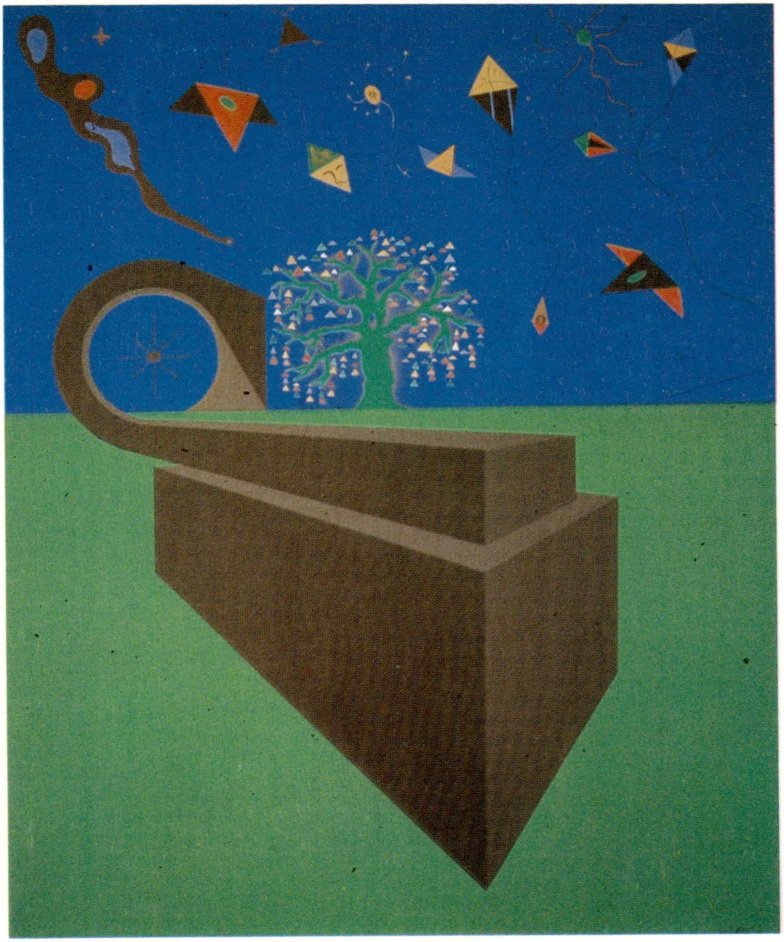

Material

Deciduous wealth, he said,
is always fresh and green.
Trusting in the cycle,
with a little stored from harvest,
winter can be weathered with confidence,–
and freedom maintained.
Minerals, on the other hand,
tend to gather dust,
can lose their lustre,
and attract thieves and fear.
They are, however, durable,
ideal for making vaults and tombs.

Human Mayflies

Mayflies
skim the surface,
skating
on water skin,
skirting lilies,
never settling.
Constant motion
prevents contact
with the heavy
element beneath.

Nectar-seeking,
they absorb nothing,
as they ricochet
from empty sweet
to sweet;
experiences
half-digested,
regurgitate
to dull the palate.

Watch them
flit on to
their potent
disillusionment.

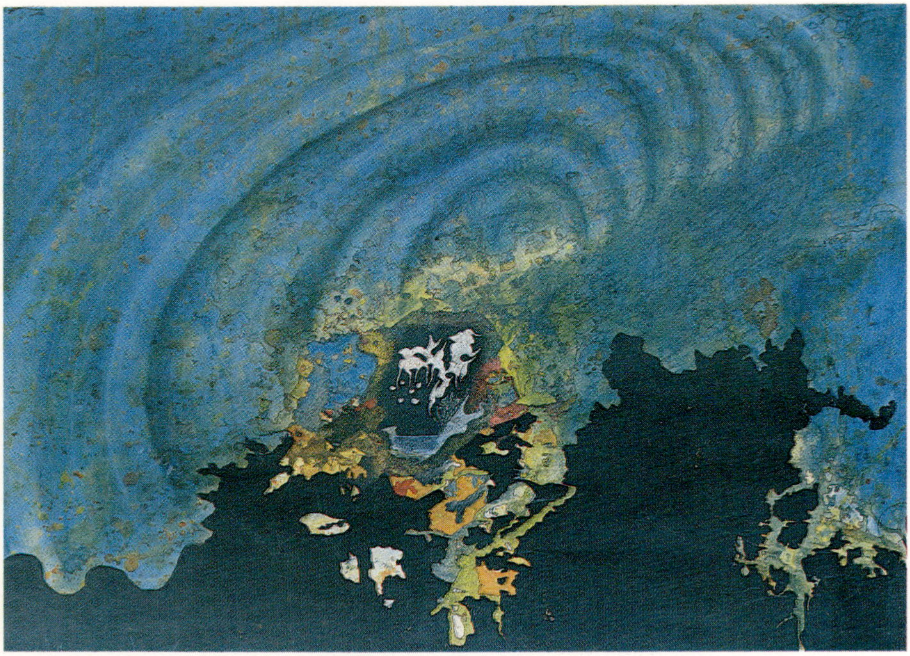

The Touch

"This is the way the world ends"?

The finger
was placed
on the throbbing pulse within the void.
Someone felt it.
The earth
shook and trembled at the touch.
It had forgotten love.
The love,
which once had spurted molten heat
to gush and pour
filling each last hidden recess,
had dried
to a dead shell,
an empty crust,
that yielded dust,
ore, and a vast material store,
but nothing more.

Then came the tears.
They froze life to the quick,
denying – even heartbeat.

But the finger
penetrated
deep and ripped
the earth apart,
until she bled,
and breathed and felt
and knew
and loved again.

                                at the top
                                a view of
                                the world

                        half way up
                        the view below
                        gives courage.

                at the beginning
                of the ascent
                insurmountable
                but challenging.

        at the foot
        daunting
        and overpowering.

    closer
    awe-inspiring
    and imposing.

In the distance
majestic.

The Mountain in Perspective

there

    are

        no

            mountains

                only

                    troughs

                        out

                            of

                                which

                                    to

                                      rise.